My Gang

Brian Moses lives in Sussex with his wife and two daughters. He travels the country presenting his poems in schools and libraries. As a child he spent half his time trying to join a gang and the other half running away from one!

Lucy Maddison lives in Balham, South London. There are three members of her gang, if Jess the cat is included.

My Gang

POEMS ABOUT FRIENDSHIP

Chosen by
Brian Moses

Illustrated by
Lucy Maddison

MACMILLAN CHILDREN'S BOOKS

For Oliver and Sophie

First published 1999
by Macmillan Children's Books
a division of Macmillan Publishers Ltd
25 Eccleston Place, London SW1W 9NF
Basingstoke and Oxford
www.macmillan.co.uk

Associated companies throughout the world

ISBN 0 330 37061 8

A CIP catalogue record for this book is available from the British Library.

Printed by Mackays of Chatham plc, Chatham, Kent.

'Break-up' by June Crebbin first published in *The Jungle Sale* by Viking Kestrel and
'What's Best' by June Crebbin first published in *Our Side of the Playground*
by the Bodley Head.

'Best Friends' by Adrian Henri first published in *The Phantom Lollipop Lady*
by Methuen Children's Books Ltd.

'Soap' by Tony Bradman first published in *Smile Please.*

'There Were These Two Girls' by Dave Ward first published in *Candy and Jazzz*
by Oxford University Press.

'Falling Out' by Ray Mather first published in *Knockout Poems* by Longman.

Contents

Samantha's Party List
John Coldwell 1

Dream Team
Frances Nagle 2

Picking Sides
Irene Rawnsley 4

Looking for a Friend
Peter Dixon 6

Get Your Things Together,
Hayley
Frances Nagle 7

Gangs
Marian Swinger 8

Mirror Games
Mick Gowar 10

Not Best Friends
Moira Andrew 12

Best of Friends
Clare Bevan 14

Blood-Brothers
Celia Warren 15

What's Best
June Crebbin 16

Compulsive Liar
Philip Waddell 18

Mutual Wish
Kate Williams 19

Soap
Tony Bradman 20

There Were These
Two Girls
Dave Ward 22

Best Friends
Adrian Henri 24

Man's Best Friend
Mike Jubb 25

Wen Egaugnal
Robin Mellor 26

Down There on the Corner
Wes Magee 28

Break-Up
June Crebbin 30

What is it?
Roger Stevens 31

Class Three's Affections
John Cotton 32

Safety in Numbers
(Count Me In)
Bernard Young 34

Amazing Grace
Andrew Fusek Peters 36

Cup Final Day 1961
Brian Moses 38

Secret Friend
John Coldwell 41

Soft Centre
Brian Moses 42

Meeting My Friend
Charles Thomson 44

Initiation
Anne Logan 46

Code
Philip Waddell 48

Falling Out
Ray Mather 49

Wanted: A Best Friend
James Carter 50

Samantha's Party List

At morning registration
A piece of paper passes
From desk to desk.
Samantha's birthday party guest list.
We've all been invited.

But in maths
Angela, Natalie and Emma
Are subtracted.

History sees
Michelle getting the chop
And Suzanne banished.

Throughout English
The list is edited.

And before RE even starts
Zoe and Faye have been excommunicated.

And halfway through geography
Carmen is sent to Coventry.

During art
Gemma is scribbled through,
Katie is rubbed out.

The end of the day,
We're all dismissed –
From the party list.

John Coldwell

Dream Team

My team
Will have all the people in it
Who're normally picked last.

Such as me.

When it's my turn to be chooser
I'll overlook Nick Magic-Feet Jones
And Supersonic Simon Hughes

And I'll point at my best friend Sean
Who'll faint with surprise
And delight.

And at Robin who's always the one
Left at the end that no one chose –
Unless he's away, in which case it's guess who?

And Tim who can't see a thing
Without his glasses.
I'll pick him.

And the rest of the guys that Mr Miller
Calls dead-legs but only need their chance
To show what they're made of.

We'll play in the cup final
In front of the class, the school, the town,
The world, the galaxy.

And due to the masterly leadership shown
By their captain, not forgetting
His three out-of-this-world goals,

We'll WIN.

Frances Nagle

Picking Sides

Why not?
He's going to be captain.
My mum's knitting him
a sweater and cap.
He'll make more runs
than you.

Want to bet?
Your captain's
just run off
with the ball!

Irene Rawnsley

Looking for a Friend

I'm looking for a best friend,
someone just like me,
someone good at football,
someone smart and free . . .
I'm seeking someone special
– quite good looking too –
someone really clever,
someone rich and true . . .
Yes – I'm looking for a new friend
   to do the things I like.
   Someone with some money,
   someone with a bike,
   someone with a pony,
   someone really new . . .
that special kind of person
   that could
   perhaps . . .
   be you?

Peter Dixon

Get Your Things Together, Hayley

Mum said the dreaded words this morning,
'Get your things together, Hayley,
We're moving.'

I've at last made a friend, and Mrs Gray
Has just stopped calling me
The New Girl.

Why do we have to go now
When I'm just beginning
To belong?

It's OK for my sister,
She's good with people.
They like her.

But I can't face the thought
Of starting all over again,
In the wrong uniform,

Knowing the wrong things,
In a class full of strangers
Who've palled up already

And don't need me.
Mum says, 'It's character-forming, Hayley.'
I say it's terribly lonely.

Frances Nagle

Gangs

They were just boys together
with no girls allowed.
They acted all tough
and went out in a crowd.
They wore scruffy jeans
on their trips to the park
where they trundled
a football around until dark.
And, chattering and giggling
(an earsplitting noise),
the girls on the swings
would make fun of the boys.

But, as the boys scornfully
sauntered away,
they knew in their hearts
girls would get them some day.

Marian Swinger

Mirror Games

If you come round to play with me
In my back garden,
And after tea
I say:
    'We'll play
    Robin Hood.
    You can be the wicked Sheriff
    Or his Captain
    (I don't mind – you choose).
    I'm Robin.
    You've got me locked in prison
    But we have a big fight
    You lose!
    Then I tie you up
    To the apple tree
    And gallop away free!'

Then that's what we should do.
It's only fair –
We're in *my* garden
And I always have the best ideas.

But if you say:
    'I'm the guest so
    I should win.
    I'll be Robin
    And you're the baddy –
    This is what happens:
    You've got me tied up,
    You're going to torture me
    But I'm too strong –

I break free!
Then I bash you on the head,
And stab you through the heart
And then you're dead!'

Then you're just being bossy,
Throwing your weight around
Again.
You're such a – *Big Head*!

Mick Gowar

Not Best Friends

Funny thing,
she didn't know how to play,
   this girl with ribbons
      in her hair.

'She's lonely,'
my mum said. 'Be nice to her.'
   Well, I tried. But it was
      tough going.

Almost silent,
we sat in the underwater gloom
   of tall spooky plants and
      half-drawn curtains.

'Do you like dolls?'
she asked. I didn't, but I nodded.
   'I've got a big dolls' house,'
      she told me.

It was huge, real
wallpaper, lights that went on and off,
   a family of four wrapped
      in tissue paper.

I put my hand inside.
'Don't touch,' she said. 'I'm not allowed
   to touch.' I stared at her,
      lost for words.

Nanny came in
with tea and cakes on a tray . 'Getting on,
   like a house on fire, I see!'
     she said brightly.

    Five o'clock chimed.
'Thank you for having me,' I said,
   remembering my manners
     just in time.

    At the door
she asked, 'Can we be best friends?'
   No way, I thought, escaping
     into the sunshine.

Moira Andrew

Best of Friends

Me and my friend
Love to fight,
Make it up
Every night.

In the playground
Every day,
Can't agree
Which game to play.

In the classroom
When we're writing
Elbows, knees
Are always fighting.

In PE and
When we're dressing,
Nudge and niggle
Every lesson.

After school and
Down the street
Grabbing bags or
Tripping feet.

Quarrel now and
Argue later.
She's my BEST friend,

And I HATE her.

Clare Bevan

Blood-Brothers

We're the best of friends.
We're pals for good.
We're blood-brothers, but
We don't like blood.
So, as tomatoes are just as red,
We're ketchup-brothers instead.

Celia Warren

What's Best

Funny how it's all right for me
To play soccer but not all right
For David to join in girls' games.
People keep saying, 'We saw you last night
With your boyfriend.' When I ignore them
They say: 'Has he kissed you?
Do you love him?'
I wish they'd leave us alone.

We like the same things. We invent
The same games. We've been friends
Ever since we both wanted the same book
In the library three years ago
And the teacher said we could share. We
Did a whole project on it. We like being together.
'When are you getting married?' people say.
I wish they'd leave us alone.

Next year they've put us in different classes,
People say it's for the best. My mum says:
'You'll be able to make friends with girls now.'
But we'll see each other at playtimes
And dinnertimes and after school and weekends.
Funny how other people always think
They know what's best.
Why can't they leave us alone?

June Crebbin

TEE
HEE —

Compulsive Liar

My best friend tells lies all the time.
He says he's lost his homework
when he hasn't even done it.
He says he's feeling sick
when he wants to bunk off school.
I've even heard him lie about his name –
when we got caught scrumping apples one time.
My friend is such a liar that he'll lie
for absolutely no reason at all.
For example if you ask him
'Do you like chocolate ice-cream?'
which everyone knows he's crazy about,
he'll automatically say 'No, I hate it.'

My dad says 'That boy's a compulsive liar,'
which means that it's so natural
for him to tell lies that he can't help it.
But yesterday something happened
which I believe shows that there is some hope for him.
Our teacher asked him who, in his opinion,
was the smartest pupil in the school.
Quick as a flash he pointed at me and said 'He is.'
I don't know why everyone laughed.

Philip Waddell

Mutual Wish

If only I was Natalie,
I'd have everything going for me.
She's a brilliant friend and we gossip no end,
but I just wish *she* was *me*.

She's quick, sly, slick, knows every trick,
makes things happen, makes life tick;

she's a joker, a mimic, a rebel, a cynic –
looks on life as one big gimmick.

She's wild and daring past all caring –
there's simply no comparing her
with cautious, mousy me.

But guess what Natalie said to me
yesterday in the dinner queue – suddenly, right out of the
    blue!
She said: 'I wish I was you.'

Kate Williams

Soap

On Monday the characters
    Turned up for school:
Sweet Karen, and Kelly,
    Whose boyfriend, Praful,
Said he'd gone off her
    In favour of Tracy
(Who *was* a bit taller,
    And rather more racy).

On Tuesday Praful had
    Some bad news to break.
Tracy, he felt,
    Had been a mistake.
It was Karen he fancied,
    His mind was quite clear.
Now Kelly *and* Tracy
    Were in floods of tears.

On Wednesday the story
    Got *very* involved.
Praful had uncovered
    A mystery to solve.
Who had sent Kelly
    A nasty, cruel note?
Tracy, said Karen –
    She wanted to gloat.

On Thursday Praful
	Announced to poor Karen
That their love was over –
	He'd found it quite barren.
Tracy, delighted,
	Told Kelly, who then
Revealed that Praful
	Was *her* boyfriend again.

On Friday the characters
	Had a big row.
The plot is in tatters,
	They're not talking now.
But tune in on Monday
	And you'll hear them speak –
This story continues,
	Same channel, next week!

Tony Bradman

There Were These Two Girls

there were these two girls
strutting down the street
whistling
loud enough to crack the windows

they were whistling
at the moon
but the moon just winked
as it hid behind a cloud

they were whistling
at the lamp-posts
but the lamp-posts just blinked
as they leaned together
like drunks

they were whistling
at the boys
who slinked off round the corner
like shamefaced puppies
with their tails between their legs

they were whistling
at the world
then they stood there listening
to see
if the world would whistle back

Dave Ward

Best Friends

It's Susan I talk to not Tracey,
Before that I sat next to Jane;
I used to be best friends with Lynda
But these days I think she's a pain.

Natasha's all right in small doses,
I meet Mandy sometimes in town;
I'm jealous of Annabel's pony
And I don't like Nicola's frown.

I used to go skating with Catherine,
Before that I went there with Ruth;
And Kate's so much better at trampoline:
She's a show-off, to tell you the truth.

I think that I'm going off Susan,
She borrowed my comb yesterday;
I think I might sit next to Tracey,
She's my nearly best friend: she's OK.

Adrian Henri

Man's Best Friend

My mum says,
'A friend in need is a friend indeed.'
But,
my Dad says,
'A friend on a lead
can get you out of the house.'

Mike Jubb

Wen Egaugnal

My friend Jeffery and I
Made up a new language.
What you had to do
was say things backwards.
So he was called Yreffej
and my little brother Yrneh.

So one rainy day
we sat in my room
and were talking
our new language.
'Evah uoy tog yna doof?'
Jeffery said.
And I said,
'Ylno emos sananab.'

Then Mum came in.
'Clear up this room, please,'
she said.
So I said,
'Tub er'ew yrev ysub.'
And she said
'What?'
and I said,
'I t'nod dnatsrednu os
I t'nac od ti.'

Well we didn't clear up,
we ate the sananab instead.

When I went downstairs
at lunch time
the table was empty.
'Mum, where's dinner?'

She just said,
'Yrros, I t'nod dnatsrednu!'

Robin Mellor

FOOW!

Down There on the Corner

Down there on the corner
at the far end of the street
hear the patter and the chatter
and the sound of stomping feet
to a blaster that is pounding out
a really funky beat
    down there on the corner
    where 'The Young Bloods' meet.

Down there on the corner
at the far end of the street
watch the boppers and the hoppers
and the dressers looking neat
as they toe-tap to the rhythms
of a throbbing sound that's sweet
    down there on the corner
    where 'The Young Bloods' meet.

Down there on the corner
at the far end of the street
all the weenies and the teenies
do the high fives when they greet
while the music goes on thumping
through the summer's dust and heat
    down there on the corner
    where 'The Young Bloods' meet.

Wes Magee

Break-Up

I've always sat next to Shirley,
And what I'd like to know
Is why's she been moved to another desk?
Why did she have to go?

It's true we sometimes argued,
And when we can't agree
It's true I've pinched her once or twice,
But the teacher didn't see.

I know we shouldn't borrow,
But I do it all the time,
And when I use her crayons and things,
Shirley doesn't mind.

I don't like this girl I'm next to,
The one in Shirley's place,
She keeps her crayons and rubbers
Zipped up in a pencil case –

And she's started this nasty rumour –
I'd like to see it proved –
I don't believe it, but *she* said
Shirley *asked* to be moved.

June Crebbin

What is it?

It's as big as the earth
and as bright as the moon
but you can't see it

It's as loud as thunder
and it plays a tune
but you can't hear it

It's as sweet as a rose
and as fresh as the dew
but you can't smell it

And it grows and grows
when I give it to you.
Can you feel it?

Friendship.

Roger Stevens

Class Three's Affections

Jim is most fond of Mary
And Mary's attracted to Joe,
While Joe thinks a lot of Rebecca
Who sits in the class's front row.

But Rebecca has thoughts about Basil,
As Basil dreams of sweet Beth,
And Beth each time she sees Ali
She finds herself quite out of breath.

Ali sends small notes to Kirsty
That hint at how much he cares,
Although Kirsty is taken with Eric
And the lovely green jacket he wears.

While Eric thinks Sita is charming,
I fear Sita thinks coolly of him.
She'd rather be liked by his classmate
The lively and oh so smart Jim.

But Jim is most fond of Mary
Which is where we began as you know,
So when it comes to affection and liking
The classroom is warm and aglow.

Yet shyness prevents them all saying,
So their secret affections aren't shared,
Except for one heart and initials
In the bike shed where somebody dared.

John Cotton

Safety in Numbers (Count Me In)

I don't seek the limelight
Don't stand centre-stage
I look and I act
Just like my mates

    I'm part of the gang
    One of the crowd
    Safe in the knowledge
    That I don't stand out

Brave in a group
Proud to belong
Surrounded by friends
I feel big and strong

    It's great to be in
    I'd hate to be out
    I'm part of the gang
    One of the crowd

Perhaps when I'm older
I won't need an army
Of identical pals
Gathered around me?

But right now . . .

    I'm part of the gang
    One of the crowd
    Secure in the knowledge
    That I don't stand out

Bernard Young

Amazing Grace

My mate Grace is totally magic,
She swallows secrets without a blink.
And when she utters dead rude spells,
She can make a bully shrink!
She's a witch of words! In a flurry of tears,
With a huff and a puff, he disappears!

My mate Grace is totally magic,
I bet she's psychic! Don't you knock it!
From over a hundred yards away,
She senses chocolate in my pocket
Even though I might be famished,
With a flash of her teeth, kaboom! It's vanished!

My mate Grace is totally magic,
Doubt disappears in the world she inhabits;
In lessons, her brain is a huge top hat,
Answers hop from her head like rabbits!
Her pen is the wand of the spelling test,
With a flourish, she conjures and comes out best.

My mate Grace is totally magic,
A witch on the pitch, she likes to tell us,
She even beats *me*, it's utterly tragic!
But she is a girl, so I can't be jealous . . .
And I'd better watch out I don't turn into a frog,
Cos she might trick me into giving her a snog!!!

Andrew Fusek Peters

Cup Final
Day 1961

Pete supported Burnley,
but Spurs were all that I cared about.
We knew, by the end of Cup Final day
that one of us would be leaping about
and one of us would be quiet,
unless, of course, it went to a replay.

So that Saturday in May
we sat down to watch
the match of the year.

And Spurs got off to a dream start
when Jimmy Greaves scored an early goal
and I was ecstatic
till Pete knocked me back, 'Sit down,'
he said, 'Shut up, watch the match.'

It was nothing much till the second half,
then Burnley scored and Pete went mad,
but just as he sat back down again
it was Bobby Smith with a cracker of a
    goal
for Spurs. 'Don't shout so much,'
my mother called, 'the teams can't hear
    you.'

Then just ten minutes before the end
Blanchflower booted a penalty
and Spurs stayed in front 3-1.

I leapt around, jumped up and down,
ran round the room holding the cup,
listened to the sound of the Wembley
crowd as I took my victory lap.

HOORAY!

3-1!

'You're daft, you are, you're crazy,'
Pete said, but I jeered him all the
way to the door.
'3-1,' I crowed, 'I told you so.'

Then, 'What shall we do tomorrow?' I called
but he didn't turn round, just walked away,
and next day too it was like a wall
had suddenly grown between us.

He kept it up for a week or so,
wouldn't speak, kept clear of me,
and it took me a week to understand
that a game of ball didn't matter at all,
it's friendship that really counts.

So I went across and knocked on Pete's door,
'I'm sorry that your team lost,' I said.
He shrugged. 'Doesn't matter any more,
there's always next year, we'll beat you
for sure.'

'I expect so,' I said,
fingers crossed
behind my back.

Brian Moses

Secret Friend

I imagined up a secret friend
From a room inside my head.
I said to him,
'Let's take a walk.'
But he beat me up instead.

John Coldwell

Soft Centre

I pull her hair,
call out names,
join in all of
my mates' rough games.

I swagger past
as she looks my way,
strong and silent,
nothing to say.

I mess about,
make out I'm tough,
but underneath
I'm soft enough.

And I'd really like
to hold her tight,
pause for a while
beneath streetlights,

buy her coffee,
talk until late,
kiss her goodnight,
tell her she's great.

But I'm meeting my mates
at the club tonight.
I couldn't do it,
it wouldn't be right.

So she smiles
And I scowl,
She speaks
And I growl.

Brian Moses

MUTTER
GROWL
GRUMBLE

Meeting my
Friend

Every day
I go to meet
my friend who lives
at the end of the street.

Sometimes we go
round the back for a walk.
Sometimes we draw
on the pavement with chalk.
Sometimes we lie
in the garden and talk.

Sometimes we raid
the deep-freeze for ice cream.
Sometimes we make
a dam in the stream.
Sometimes we join
with the rest of the team –

behind the garage –
for a game of football.
Sometimes we go
upstairs and play pool.
Sometimes there's nothing
to do at all,

but even then
I go to meet
my friend who lives
at the end of the street.

Charles Thomson

Initiation

When our ball was kicked over the wall by Jack,
We found that his neighbour wouldn't give it back,
So Billy and Jack and Matthew and me,
All had a meeting under a tree,
Billy said, 'Dare you!' Matthew said, 'Try!'
Jack said, 'You can't do it!' and I said, 'Can't I?'
'Just watch me!' I said, and with great panache,
Over that wall I took a mad dash!
With adrenaline pumping – was I breaking the law?
I jumped in the garden of the old man next door.
Crept round behind a pile of logs,
Then I nearly died – there were his dogs!
Lying there, dozing, quite catatonic,
Then, the next minute, they became supersonic!
Snapping and snarling, they began to give chase,
So I grabbed the ball and started to race!
With the dogs at my heels (and growling at that)
I made it to where Jack, Billy and Matt
Were shouting and cheering, hanging over the wall,
They dragged me to safety – clutching the ball!
Then as from the top of that wall I sprang
I gasped, '*Now* – let me be part of your gang?'

Anne Logan

Code

My best friend and I have a code.
I don't know who gave it to him but now I've picked it
    up.

All I had to do was to learn to speak backwards.
Won I wonk woh s'ti sa ysae sa gnillaf ffo a gol.

We speak like this when we don't want
others to understand what we're saying.

(At first I thought it was a horrid code
but now that I've got used to it it's as easy as CBA.)

Lately we've been hanging around with some other kids
and I'm worried in case they pick it up.

Actually I'd really prefer it if you weren't exposed to this
    poem
or you might get our code too.

Philip Waddell

Falling Out

James and I
Fell out this morning;
Nothing else matters.
The teacher is talking
But I don't hear.
Giving out exam results,
But I don't care.
Rain lashes the window –
I forgot my coat –
Even the weather is against me.
The bell rings.
We go to the next lesson.
He goes with the crowd,
Laughing too loud.
I go alone.

Ray Mather

Wanted:
A Best Friend

Interested? Just fill in your details below

Job Title – My best friend.

Duties – To hang out with me. To tell me *everything*. To be brilliant. And very funny. But not quite as funny as me.

Salary – The pleasure of my company. What more could you ask for?!?

Name:

Age: (Infants and boys need *not* apply)

Hobbies: (If you're about to write 'stamp collecting' or 'knitting' or 'jigsaw puzzles', forget it.)

Previous Best Friends: (I'll find out if you're fibbing.)

Best Subjects: (Must not be PE or art. These are mine. If you like maths, or even worse, if you're good at it, stop writing this instant.)

Now answer these questions:
Have you ever sneaked on a friend? (A brother or sister doesn't count.)
How secret is a secret?

What is your favourite soap on TV? (Careful how you answer this one.)

What is your favourite pop group?

What do you think of Miss? (No, really.)

And now, in your own words, say why it would be fantastic to be best friends with me and why you think you think you'd be good at the job:

Finish off this phrase: All teachers are very sad because . . .

Please **RSVP** (reply)
ASAP (as soon as possible)
With a **SAE** (stamped addressed envelope)
To **ME** (yes, me!!)

James Carter

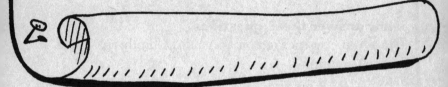

I'm Telling On You

Poems about brothers and sisters
Chosen by Brian Moses

Where Are They?

'You've got your brother's hair!'
Said Auntie Claire.

'You've got your sister's nose!'
Said Auntie Rose.

I shook my head.

'Not me,' I said,
'I haven't touched them –
Honest!'

Trevor Harvey

Mini Beasts

Poems chosen by Brian Moses

Mobile Home for Sale

Judy is a delightful
Mobile Home
with Central Heating
a warm Basement
superb Penthouse views
and includes luxury
Deep Pile Carpets
in black and white.
Fully Air-Conditioned
by large wagging tail.
This Border Collie
would suit large family of fleas.

Roger Stevens

Ridiculous Relatives

Poems chosen by Paul Cookson

Auntie Betty Thinks She's Batgirl

Auntie Betty pulls her cloak on
And the mask – the one with ears.
Almost ready, check the lipstick,
Wait until the neighbours cheer.
Through the window. What a leap!
She lands right in the driver's seat.
Off she goes with style and grace
To make our world a better place.

Andrea Shavick

A selected list of poetry books available from Macmillan

The prices shown below are correct at the time of going to press. However, Macmillan Publishers reserve the right to show new retail prices on covers which may differ from those previously advertised.

The Secret Lives of Teachers
Revealing rhymes, chosen by Brian Moses   0 330 34265 7   £3.50

More Secret Lives of Teachers
More revealing rhymes, chosen by Brian Moses   0 330 34994 5   £3.50

Aliens Stole My Underpants
And other intergalactic poems,
chosen by Brian Moses   0 330 34995 3   £2.99

Parent-Free Zone
Poems about parents, chosen by Brian Moses   0 330 34554 0   £2.99

Don't Look at Me in That Tone of Voice
Poems by Brian Moses   0 330 35337 3   £2.99

School Trips
Poems chosen by Brian Moses   0 330 35279 2   £2.99

We Three Kings
Poems chosen by Brian Moses   0 330 37055 3   £2.99

All Macmillan titles can be ordered at your local bookshop or are available by post from:

Book Service by Post
PO Box 29, Douglas, Isle of Man IM99 1BQ

Credit cards accepted. For details:
Telephone: 01624 675137
Fax: 01624 670923
E-mail: bookshop@enterprise.net

Free postage and packing in the UK.
Overseas customers: add £1 per book (paperback)
and £3 per book (hardback).